AF316691

Daily Practice of Manifestation

369
MANIFESTATION
JOURNAL
BOOK

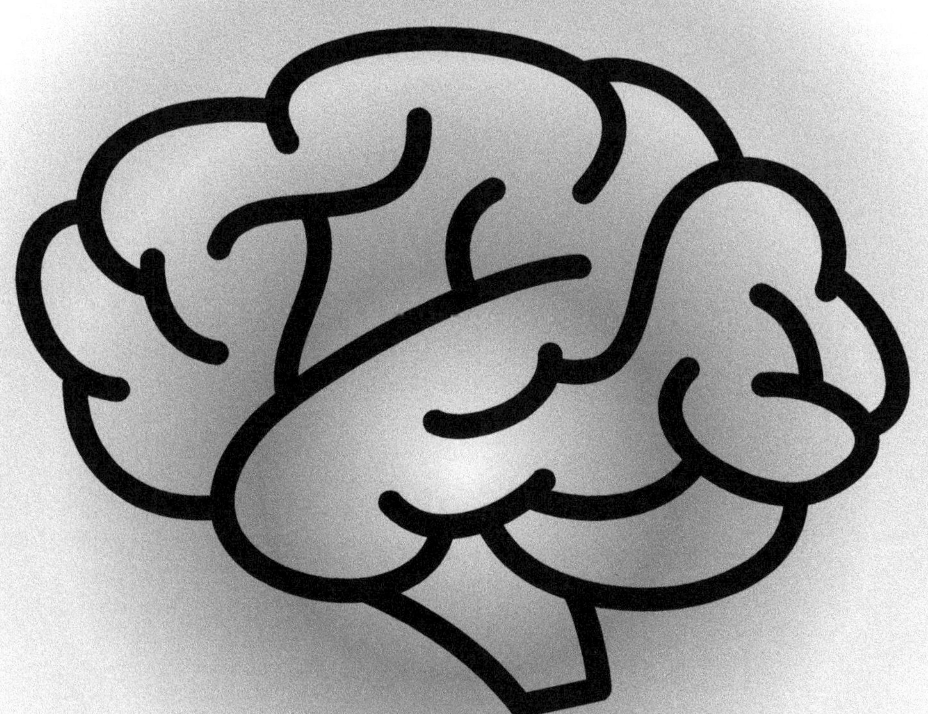

BROSSBEE PUBLISHING

Thank You Universe,

I am ___________________________
Committing myself and taking the responsibility to
say thank you/grateful for whatever I have/will be in
my life, and I am doing this affirmation practice to
manifest my dream life

Create Your Positive Thought, Create your Abundant life

"If you can change your thoughts, then you can change anything"

About This Journal

This journal is about a 369 manifestation method to attract your dreams and practice the law of attraction every day in your life.

Align your brain in the right way to increase the positive vibration of your body.

369 is the Universal number which is used for abundance and prosperity in every aspect of your life.

This number was brought into the view of the world by the Scientist Nikola Tesla to show the power of these numbers.

This number also comes into the Angel numbers for wishing and asking for help from angels.

It is 369 Journaling for the manifestation of the exact things in your life by writing your dreams repeatedly for a certain period.

This Journal will help you to create a positive mindset toward life and increase the chances of better visualization and manifestation of your dreams and your quality of life.

What is Affirmation?

Affirmation is a positive sentence which use to align your brain in a positive direction to increase the positive vibration and dedicate your thought in one direction to manifest your desire.

Affirmations in New Thought and New Age terminology refer primarily to the practice of positive thinking and self-empowerment —fostering a belief that "a positive mental attitude supported by affirmations will achieve success in anything." -- Wikipedia

How to Use this Journal?

This journal is divided into multiple parts for your different Wishes or Dreams. Always follow the sample affirmation from the 369 Affirmation page of Day 0 to write your affirmations properly.

you should need to write your single affirmation in 3 different parts morning, noon and night frequently like 3 times in the morning, 6 times at noon and 9 times at night every day for 21 days consistently with a different interval of time in a whole day as per your convenience.

This journal is created for a set of 21 days of a challenge for 3 attempts, where you can repeat your dream affirmation for 21 days then another for another 21 days.

Every part where you can write a unique and separate affirmation for a specific thing. your dreams are always divided into 4 areas of life health, money, career and relationships. You need to balance all these 4 to achieve and maintain happiness in life.

Write you one dream at a time and focus on only one thing write it, feel it, and visualized it like what you already achieved

This journal contains multiple sections for multiple dreams, so let's give it the try to uplift your vibration and manifest your dream easily.

369 Affirmation Sample

3 — **3 times Same Affirmation (Morning)**

1. I am already making $12000 every month happily and easily
2. I am already making $12000 every month happily and easily
3. I am already making $12000 every month happily and easily

6 — **6 times Same Affirmation (Afternoon)**

1. I am already making $12000 every month happily and easily
2. I am already making $12000 every month happily and easily
3. I am already making $12000 every month happily and easily
4. I am already making $12000 every month happily and easily
5. I am already making $12000 every month happily and easily
6. I am already making $12000 every month happily and easily

9

9 times Same Affirmation
(Evening or Night)

1. I am already making $12000 every month happily and easily

2. I am already making $12000 every month happily and easily

3. I am already making $12000 every month happily and easily

4. I am already making $12000 every month happily and easily

5. I am already making $12000 every month happily and easily

6. I am already making $12000 every month happily and easily

7. I am already making $12000 every month happily and easily

8. I am already making $12000 every month happily and easily

9. I am already making $12000 every month happily and easily

Note: While Writing your affirmation in 3 different steps make sure that you feel each affirmation like you already have that.

#1
21-Days Challenge

START YOUR DAILY CHALLENGE OF 369 JOURNALING

369 Affirmation Day__

DATE:

3

3 times Same Affirmation (Morning)

1.
2.
3.

6

6 time Same Affirmation (Afternoon)

1.
2.
3.
4.
5.
6.

9   9 time Same Affirmation
(Evening or Night)

1.

2.

3.

4.

5.

6.

7.

8.

9.

369 Affirmation Day__

3 — 3 times Same Affirmation (Morning)

1.
2.
3.

6 — 6 time Same Affirmation (Afternoon)

1.
2.
3.
4.
5.
6.

9   9 time Same Affirmation (Evening or Night)

1. ....

2. ....

3. ....

4. ....

5. ....

6. ....

7. ....

8. ....

9. ....

369 Affirmation Day__

3

**3 times Same Affirmation
(Morning)**

1.
2.
3.

6

**6 time Same Affirmation
(Afternoon)**

1.
2.
3.
4.
5.
6.

9

9 time Same Affirmation
(Evening or Night)

1. ________________________________

2. ________________________________

3. ________________________________

4. ________________________________

5. ________________________________

6. ________________________________

7. ________________________________

8. ________________________________

9. ________________________________

369 Affirmation Day__

DATE:

---

3 — **3 times Same Affirmation (Morning)**

1.
2.
3.

---

6 — **6 time Same Affirmation (Afternoon)**

1.
2.
3.
4.
5.
6.

9

9 time Same Affirmation
(Evening or Night)

1. ....

2. ....

3. ....

4. ....

5. ....

6. ....

7. ....

8. ....

9. ....

369 Affirmation Day__

3   3 times Same Affirmation (Morning)

1. ....
2. ....
3. ....

6   6 time Same Affirmation (Afternoon)

1. ....
2. ....
3. ....
4. ....
5. ....
6. ....

9

9 time Same Affirmation
(Evening or Night)

1. ....

2. ....

3. ....

4. ....

5. ....

6. ....

7. ....

8. ....

9. ....

369 Affirmation Day__

3 — 3 times Same Affirmation (Morning)

1.
2.
3.

6 — 6 time Same Affirmation (Afternoon)

1.
2.
3.
4.
5.
6.

9

9 time Same Affirmation
(Evening or Night)

1. ____

2. ____

3. ____

4. ____

5. ____

6. ____

7. ____

8. ____

9. ____

369 Affirmation Day__

3 3 times Same Affirmation
(Morning)

1.
2.
3.

6 6 time Same Affirmation
(Afternoon)

1.
2.
3.
4.
5.
6.

9

9 time Same Affirmation
(Evening or Night)

1. ....

2. ....

3. ....

4. ....

5. ....

6. ....

7. ....

8. ....

9. ....

369 Affirmation Day__

3 — 3 times Same Affirmation (Morning)

1.
2.
3.

6 — 6 time Same Affirmation (Afternoon)

1.
2.
3.
4.
5.
6.

9

9 time Same Affirmation
(Evening or Night)

1. ....

2. ....

3. ....

4. ....

5. ....

6. ....

7. ....

8. ....

9. ....

369 Affirmation Day__

DATE:

3 — 3 times Same Affirmation (Morning)

1.
2.
3.

6 — 6 time Same Affirmation (Afternoon)

1.
2.
3.
4.
5.
6.

9

9 time Same Affirmation
(Evening or Night)

1. ____

2. ____

3. ____

4. ____

5. ____

6. ____

7. ____

8. ____

9. ____

369 Affirmation Day__

DATE:

3 **3 times Same Affirmation (Morning)**

1. _______________
2. _______________
3. _______________

6 **6 time Same Affirmation (Afternoon)**

1. _______________
2. _______________
3. _______________
4. _______________
5. _______________
6. _______________

9

9 time Same Affirmation
(Evening or Night)

1. ....

2. ....

3. ....

4. ....

5. ....

6. ....

7. ....

8. ....

9. ....

369 Affirmation Day__

3 — 3 times Same Affirmation (Morning)

1.
2.
3.

6 — 6 time Same Affirmation (Afternoon)

1.
2.
3.
4.
5.
6.

9

9 time Same Affirmation
(Evening or Night)

1. ....

2. ....

3. ....

4. ....

5. ....

6. ....

7. ....

8. ....

9. ....

369 Affirmation Day__

DATE:

3 — 3 times Same Affirmation (Morning)

1.
2.
3.

6 — 6 time Same Affirmation (Afternoon)

1.
2.
3.
4.
5.
6.

9

9 time Same Affirmation
(Evening or Night)

1. ____

2. ____

3. ____

4. ____

5. ____

6. ____

7. ____

8. ____

9. ____

369 Affirmation Day__

3 — **3 times Same Affirmation (Morning)**

1.
2.
3.

6 — **6 time Same Affirmation (Afternoon)**

1.
2.
3.
4.
5.
6.

9

9 time Same Affirmation
(Evening or Night)

1. ....

2. ....

3. ....

4. ....

5. ....

6. ....

7. ....

8. ....

9. ....

369 Affirmation Day__

DATE:

| 3 | 3 times Same Affirmation (Morning) |

1.
2.
3.

| 6 | 6 time Same Affirmation (Afternoon) |

1.
2.
3.
4.
5.
6.

9

9 time Same Affirmation
(Evening or Night)

1.
2.
3.
4.
5.
6.
7.
8.
9.

369 Affirmation Day__

DATE:

3 — 3 times Same Affirmation (Morning)

1. ....
2. ....
3. ....

6 — 6 time Same Affirmation (Afternoon)

1. ....
2. ....
3. ....
4. ....
5. ....
6. ....

9

9 time Same Affirmation
(Evening or Night)

1.

2.

3.

4.

5.

6.

7.

8.

9.

369 Affirmation Day__

DATE:

3 3 times Same Affirmation (Morning)

1.
2.
3.

6 6 time Same Affirmation (Afternoon)

1.
2.
3.
4.
5.
6.

9

9 time Same Affirmation
(Evening or Night)

1. ____

2. ____

3. ____

4. ____

5. ____

6. ____

7. ____

8. ____

9. ____

369 Affirmation Day___

3

3 times Same Affirmation (Morning)

1.
2.
3.

6

6 time Same Affirmation (Afternoon)

1.
2.
3.
4.
5.
6.

9

9 time Same Affirmation
(Evening or Night)

1. ....

2. ....

3. ....

4. ....

5. ....

6. ....

7. ....

8. ....

9. ....

369 Affirmation Day__

3 — 3 times Same Affirmation (Morning)

1. ....
2. ....
3. ....

6 — 6 time Same Affirmation (Afternoon)

1. ....
2. ....
3. ....
4. ....
5. ....
6. ....

9

9 time Same Affirmation
(Evening or Night)

1.

2.

3.

4.

5.

6.

7.

8.

9.

369 Affirmation Day__

3 — 3 times Same Affirmation (Morning)

1.
2.
3.

6 — 6 time Same Affirmation (Afternoon)

1.
2.
3.
4.
5.
6.

9

9 time Same Affirmation
(Evening or Night)

1.
2.
3.
4.
5.
6.
7.
8.
9.

369 Affirmation Day__

3 — 3 times Same Affirmation (Morning)

1.
2.
3.

6 — 6 time Same Affirmation (Afternoon)

1.
2.
3.
4.
5.
6.

9

9 time Same Affirmation
(Evening or Night)

1. ....

2. ....

3. ....

4. ....

5. ....

6. ....

7. ....

8. ....

9. ....

369 Affirmation Day___

DATE:

3 — 3 times Same Affirmation (Morning)

1. ....
2. ....
3. ....

6 — 6 time Same Affirmation (Afternoon)

1. ....
2. ....
3. ....
4. ....
5. ....
6. ....

9

9 time Same Affirmation
(Evening or Night)

1.

2.

3.

4.

5.

6.

7.

8.

9.

#2
21-Days Challenge

START YOUR DAILY CHALLENGE OF 369 JOURNALING

369 Affirmation Day___

3 — 3 times Same Affirmation (Morning)

1.
2.
3.

6 — 6 time Same Affirmation (Afternoon)

1.
2.
3.
4.
5.
6.

9

9 time Same Affirmation
(Evening or Night)

1. ....

2. ....

3. ....

4. ....

5. ....

6. ....

7. ....

8. ....

9. ....

369 Affirmation Day__

3 — 3 times Same Affirmation (Morning)

1.
2.
3.

6 — 6 time Same Affirmation (Afternoon)

1.
2.
3.
4.
5.
6.

9

9 time Same Affirmation
(Evening or Night)

1. ....

2. ....

3. ....

4. ....

5. ....

6. ....

7. ....

8. ....

9. ....

369 Affirmation Day__

---

3 — 3 times Same Affirmation (Morning)

1.
2.
3.

---

6 — 6 time Same Affirmation (Afternoon)

1.
2.
3.
4.
5.
6.

9 time Same Affirmation
(Evening or Night)

1. ....

2. ....

3. ....

4. ....

5. ....

6. ....

7. ....

8. ....

9. ....

369 Affirmation Day___

3 **3 times Same Affirmation (Morning)**

1.
2.
3.

6 **6 time Same Affirmation (Afternoon)**

1.
2.
3.
4.
5.
6.

9

9 time Same Affirmation
(Evening or Night)

1.

2.

3.

4.

5.

6.

7.

8.

9.

369 Affirmation Day___

DATE:

3 — 3 times Same Affirmation (Morning)

1.
2.
3.

6 — 6 time Same Affirmation (Afternoon)

1.
2.
3.
4.
5.
6.

9

9 time Same Affirmation
(Evening or Night)

1.

2.

3.

4.

5.

6.

7.

8.

9.

369 Affirmation Day__

DATE:

3 — 3 times Same Affirmation (Morning)

1.
2.
3.

6 — 6 time Same Affirmation (Afternoon)

1.
2.
3.
4.
5.
6.

9

9 time Same Affirmation
(Evening or Night)

1. ....

2. ....

3. ....

4. ....

5. ....

6. ....

7. ....

8. ....

9. ....

369 Affirmation Day__

DATE:

---

3 — **3 times Same Affirmation (Morning)**

1.
2.
3.

---

6 — **6 time Same Affirmation (Afternoon)**

1.
2.
3.
4.
5.
6.

9

9 time Same Affirmation
(Evening or Night)

1. ....

2. ....

3. ....

4. ....

5. ....

6. ....

7. ....

8. ....

9. ....

369 Affirmation Day__

3

3 times Same Affirmation (Morning)

1. ....
2. ....
3. ....

6

6 time Same Affirmation (Afternoon)

1. ....
2. ....
3. ....
4. ....
5. ....
6. ....

9

9 time Same Affirmation
(Evening or Night)

1.

2.

3.

4.

5.

6.

7.

8.

9.

369 Affirmation Day__

3   3 times Same Affirmation (Morning)

1.
2.
3.

6   6 time Same Affirmation (Afternoon)

1.
2.
3.
4.
5.
6.

9

9 time Same Affirmation
(Evening or Night)

1.

2.

3.

4.

5.

6.

7.

8.

9.

369 Affirmation Day__

3   3 times Same Affirmation (Morning)

1.
2.
3.

6   6 time Same Affirmation (Afternoon)

1.
2.
3.
4.
5.
6.

9

9 time Same Affirmation
(Evening or Night)

1. ....

2. ....

3. ....

4. ....

5. ....

6. ....

7. ....

8. ....

9. ....

369 Affirmation Day__

---

3   3 times Same Affirmation
(Morning)

1. ....
2. ....
3. ....

---

6   6 time Same Affirmation
(Afternoon)

1. ....
2. ....
3. ....
4. ....
5. ....
6. ....

9

9 time Same Affirmation
(Evening or Night)

1. ....

2. ....

3. ....

4. ....

5. ....

6. ....

7. ....

8. ....

9. ....

369 Affirmation Day__

3 — 3 times Same Affirmation (Morning)

1.
2.
3.

6 — 6 time Same Affirmation (Afternoon)

1.
2.
3.
4.
5.
6.

9

9 time Same Affirmation
(Evening or Night)

1. ____

2. ____

3. ____

4. ____

5. ____

6. ____

7. ____

8. ____

9. ____

369 Affirmation Day__

3 — 3 times Same Affirmation (Morning)

1.
2.
3.

6 — 6 time Same Affirmation (Afternoon)

1.
2.
3.
4.
5.
6.

9

9 time Same Affirmation
(Evening or Night)

1. ....

2. ....

3. ....

4. ....

5. ....

6. ....

7. ....

8. ....

9. ....

369 Affirmation
Day__

3   **3 times Same Affirmation**
(Morning)

1.
2.
3.

6   **6 time Same Affirmation**
(Afternoon)

1.
2.
3.
4.
5.
6.

9

9 time Same Affirmation
(Evening or Night)

1. ....

2. ....

3. ....

4. ....

5. ....

6. ....

7. ....

8. ....

9. ....

369 Affirmation Day___

3 — **3 times Same Affirmation (Morning)**

1.
2.
3.

6 — **6 time Same Affirmation (Afternoon)**

1.
2.
3.
4.
5.
6.

9

9 time Same Affirmation
(Evening or Night)

1.

2.

3.

4.

5.

6.

7.

8.

9.

369 Affirmation Day__

3

3 times Same Affirmation (Morning)

1. ....
2. ....
3. ....

6

6 time Same Affirmation (Afternoon)

1. ....
2. ....
3. ....
4. ....
5. ....
6. ....

9

9 time Same Affirmation
(Evening or Night)

1.

2.

3.

4.

5.

6.

7.

8.

9.

369 Affirmation Day__

3 — 3 times Same Affirmation (Morning)

1.
2.
3.

6 — 6 time Same Affirmation (Afternoon)

1.
2.
3.
4.
5.
6.

9

9 time Same Affirmation
(Evening or Night)

1. ....

2. ....

3. ....

4. ....

5. ....

6. ....

7. ....

8. ....

9. ....

369 Affirmation Day__

3   3 times Same Affirmation (Morning)

1. ....
2. ....
3. ....

6   6 time Same Affirmation (Afternoon)

1. ....
2. ....
3. ....
4. ....
5. ....
6. ....

9

9 time Same Affirmation
(Evening or Night)

1. ____

2. ____

3. ____

4. ____

5. ____

6. ____

7. ____

8. ____

9. ____

369 Affirmation Day___

3 — 3 times Same Affirmation (Morning)

1.
2.
3.

6 — 6 time Same Affirmation (Afternoon)

1.
2.
3.
4.
5.
6.

9

9 time Same Affirmation
(Evening or Night)

1. ....

2. ....

3. ....

4. ....

5. ....

6. ....

7. ....

8. ....

9. ....

369 Affirmation Day___

3 — 3 times Same Affirmation (Morning)

1.
2.
3.

6 — 6 time Same Affirmation (Afternoon)

1.
2.
3.
4.
5.
6.

9

**9 time Same Affirmation
(Evening or Night)**

1. ....

2. ....

3. ....

4. ....

5. ....

6. ....

7. ....

8. ....

9. ....

369 Affirmation Day__

DATE:

3 — 3 times Same Affirmation (Morning)

1.
2.
3.

6 — 6 time Same Affirmation (Afternoon)

1.
2.
3.
4.
5.
6.

9

9 time Same Affirmation
(Evening or Night)

1.

2.

3.

4.

5.

6.

7.

8.

9.

#3
21-Days Challenge

START YOUR
DAILY
CHALLENGE OF
369 JOURNALING

369 Affirmation Day__

DATE:

3 — 3 times Same Affirmation (Morning)

1.
2.
3.

6 — 6 time Same Affirmation (Afternoon)

1.
2.
3.
4.
5.
6.

9

9 time Same Affirmation
(Evening or Night)

1. ....

2. ....

3. ....

4. ....

5. ....

6. ....

7. ....

8. ....

9. ....

369 Affirmation Day__

3   3 times Same Affirmation (Morning)

1.
2.
3.

6   6 time Same Affirmation (Afternoon)

1.
2.
3.
4.
5.
6.

9

9 time Same Affirmation
(Evening or Night)

1. ....

2. ....

3. ....

4. ....

5. ....

6. ....

7. ....

8. ....

9. ....

369 Affirmation Day__

3 — 3 times Same Affirmation
(Morning)

1.
2.
3.

6 — 6 time Same Affirmation
(Afternoon)

1.
2.
3.
4.
5.
6.

9

9 time Same Affirmation
(Evening or Night)

1. ....

2. ....

3. ....

4. ....

5. ....

6. ....

7. ....

8. ....

9. ....

369 Affirmation Day__

DATE:

---

3 — 3 times Same Affirmation (Morning)

1.
2.
3.

---

6 — 6 time Same Affirmation (Afternoon)

1.
2.
3.
4.
5.
6.

9

9 time Same Affirmation
(Evening or Night)

1. ....

2. ....

3. ....

4. ....

5. ....

6. ....

7. ....

8. ....

9. ....

369 Affirmation Day___

3   3 times Same Affirmation (Morning)

1. ....
2. ....
3. ....

6   6 time Same Affirmation (Afternoon)

1. ....
2. ....
3. ....
4. ....
5. ....
6. ....

9

9 time Same Affirmation
(Evening or Night)

1. ....

2. ....

3. ....

4. ....

5. ....

6. ....

7. ....

8. ....

9. ....

369 Affirmation Day__

DATE:

---

3 — 3 times Same Affirmation
(Morning)

1.
2.
3.

---

6 — 6 time Same Affirmation
(Afternoon)

1.
2.
3.
4.
5.
6.

9

9 time Same Affirmation
(Evening or Night)

1. ____

2. ____

3. ____

4. ____

5. ____

6. ____

7. ____

8. ____

9. ____

369 Affirmation Day__

---

3 **3 times Same Affirmation (Morning)**

1.
2.
3.

---

6 **6 time Same Affirmation (Afternoon)**

1.
2.
3.
4.
5.
6.

9

9 time Same Affirmation
(Evening or Night)

1. ....

2. ....

3. ....

4. ....

5. ....

6. ....

7. ....

8. ....

9. ....

369 Affirmation Day__

3 3 times Same Affirmation (Morning)

1.
2.
3.

6 6 time Same Affirmation (Afternoon)

1.
2.
3.
4.
5.
6.

9   9 time Same Affirmation
(Evening or Night)

1. ....

2. ....

3. ....

4. ....

5. ....

6. ....

7. ....

8. ....

9. ....

369 Affirmation Day__

3 — 3 times Same Affirmation (Morning)

1.
2.
3.

6 — 6 time Same Affirmation (Afternoon)

1.
2.
3.
4.
5.
6.

9

9 time Same Affirmation
(Evening or Night)

1. ____

2. ____

3. ____

4. ____

5. ____

6. ____

7. ____

8. ____

9. ____

369 Affirmation Day__

DATE:

3

3 times Same Affirmation (Morning)

1.
2.
3.

6

6 time Same Affirmation (Afternoon)

1.
2.
3.
4.
5.
6.

9

9 time Same Affirmation
(Evening or Night)

1. ....

2. ....

3. ....

4. ....

5. ....

6. ....

7. ....

8. ....

9. ....

369 Affirmation Day__

DATE:

---

3 — **3 times Same Affirmation (Morning)**

1. ____
2. ____
3. ____

---

6 — **6 time Same Affirmation (Afternoon)**

1. ____
2. ____
3. ____
4. ____
5. ____
6. ____

9

9 time Same Affirmation
(Evening or Night)

1.

2.

3.

4.

5.

6.

7.

8.

9.

369 Affirmation Day__

3 — 3 times Same Affirmation (Morning)

1.
2.
3.

6 — 6 time Same Affirmation (Afternoon)

1.
2.
3.
4.
5.
6.

9

9 time Same Affirmation
(Evening or Night)

1. ....

2. ....

3. ....

4. ....

5. ....

6. ....

7. ....

8. ....

9. ....

369 Affirmation Day__

DATE:

---

3 — 3 times Same Affirmation (Morning)

1.
2.
3.

---

6 — 6 time Same Affirmation (Afternoon)

1.
2.
3.
4.
5.
6.

9

9 time Same Affirmation
(Evening or Night)

1.

2.

3.

4.

5.

6.

7.

8.

9.

369 Affirmation Day__

DATE:

---

3 — **3 times Same Affirmation (Morning)**

1.
2.
3.

---

6 — **6 time Same Affirmation (Afternoon)**

1.
2.
3.
4.
5.
6.

9   9 time Same Affirmation
(Evening or Night)

1. ....

2. ....

3. ....

4. ....

5. ....

6. ....

7. ....

8. ....

9. ....

369 Affirmation Day__

3 — 3 times Same Affirmation (Morning)

1.
2.
3.

6 — 6 time Same Affirmation (Afternoon)

1.
2.
3.
4.
5.
6.

9

9 time Same Affirmation
(Evening or Night)

1. ....

2. ....

3. ....

4. ....

5. ....

6. ....

7. ....

8. ....

9. ....

369 Affirmation Day__

3

3 times Same Affirmation (Morning)

1.
2.
3.

6

6 time Same Affirmation (Afternoon)

1.
2.
3.
4.
5.
6.

9

9 time Same Affirmation
(Evening or Night)

1.

2.

3.

4.

5.

6.

7.

8.

9.

369 Affirmation Day__

3 — **3 times Same Affirmation (Morning)**

1.
2.
3.

6 — **6 time Same Affirmation (Afternoon)**

1.
2.
3.
4.
5.
6.

9

9 time Same Affirmation
(Evening or Night)

1. ....

2. ....

3. ....

4. ....

5. ....

6. ....

7. ....

8. ....

9. ....

369 Affirmation Day__

DATE:

---

3 — 3 times Same Affirmation (Morning)

1.
2.
3.

---

6 — 6 time Same Affirmation (Afternoon)

1.
2.
3.
4.
5.
6.

9

9 time Same Affirmation
(Evening or Night)

1.

2.

3.

4.

5.

6.

7.

8.

9.

369 Affirmation Day__

DATE:

3 — 3 times Same Affirmation (Morning)

1.
2.
3.

6 — 6 time Same Affirmation (Afternoon)

1.
2.
3.
4.
5.
6.

9

9 time Same Affirmation
(Evening or Night)

1. ....

2. ....

3. ....

4. ....

5. ....

6. ....

7. ....

8. ....

9. ....

369 Affirmation Day__

DATE:

3 — 3 times Same Affirmation (Morning)

1.
2.
3.

6 — 6 time Same Affirmation (Afternoon)

1.
2.
3.
4.
5.
6.

9

9 time Same Affirmation
(Evening or Night)

1.

2.

3.

4.

5.

6.

7.

8.

9.

369 Affirmation Day__

---

3 — 3 times Same Affirmation (Morning)

1. ....
2. ....
3. ....

---

6 — 6 time Same Affirmation (Afternoon)

1. ....
2. ....
3. ....
4. ....
5. ....
6. ....

9

9 time Same Affirmation
(Evening or Night)

1.

2.

3.

4.

5.

6.

7.

8.

9.